"Poetry cannot best death. But poetry can make the best of it. 'I need an answer. There are no answers,' wisely writes Mitchell Untch. This talented poet pens a thesaurus of longing with his first book. His lyrics multiply with the nuances of loss: mainly the speaker's twin from AIDS, but also the loss of a platonic Midwestern girlfriend—I've never read of this kind of unseen love in a more definitive manner. Editors were 'floored' by these poems. Little wonder. Reader, be floored."

—Spencer Reece, author of *The Clerk's Tale*

"The focus of Mitchell Untch's stunning debut collection, *Memorial With Liminial Space*, pivots on leaving, leaving behind, having left, the undiscovered treasure or detritus. With gorgeous imagery, the poet searches for answers where there are none available—in nurses' stations, carnival booths, bodies of lovers, the past. Even Ronnie and Nancy Reagan, turn away in 1980's AID's pandemic blindness. Too much pain. Too much exquisite pain. As he writes in "Better Angels II," 'No one was listening, and we had become fewer and less, / voices like brooms over sidewalks.' If reason needs to find its way, the poems in *Memorial With Liminal Space* unearth a hidden pathway within. El Dorado. Atlantis. Shangri La. Eden."

—Laurel Ann Bogen, author of *The Misread City* and
winner of the Academy of American Poets Award

"The gorgeous and moving poems of Mitchell Untch's *Memorial with Liminal Space* begin by looking back unflinchingly at the suffering and death of his twin brother from the HIV virus. We follow this poet as he laments through the "corridors of grief." And as he continues to journey into rooms and scenes from his past, he discovers he can cast a new, prismatic light on those dark moments, turning despair into grace and beauty. Mitchell Untch demonstrates, with his attentiveness to sensual details, how much there is to celebrate and sing: 'the hummingbird's / bright delving, a wakefulness that / cannot be described except that / it lives.'"

—Molly Bendall, author of *Watchful*

MEMORIAL WITH LIMINAL SPACE

Mitchell Untch

DRIFTWOOD
PRESS

Independently published by *Driftwood Press*
in the United States of America.

Managing Poetry Editor & Interviewer: Jerrod Schwarz
Poetry Editor: Andrew Hemmert
Cover Image: Caspar David Friedrich
Cover Design: Sally Franckowiak & Jerrod Schwarz
Interior Design: Jerrod Schwarz
Copyeditor: Jerrod Schwarz & James McNulty
Fonts: Merriweather & Alternate Gothic Extra Condensed

First published May 30th, 2023
ISBN-13: 978-1-949065-25-1

Please visit our website at www.driftwoodpress.com
or email us at editor@driftwoodpress.net.

Contents

coda iii

coda iv

coda v

for my twin brother, Dana,
and Richard C. Lancaster

Psalm

for the unuttered word extravagant frames of light
        the lost son for a door slammed shut for abbreviation's deftness
and windowless rooms grass slowly dying on the lawn
        the ibis the sea turtle for the white wrapped wingspan of a swan
the shadow of memory the ripening rage the stopped clock
        for mending the mind the burning cloth the dark plumage
of a library shelf for its paper boat of words a sudden flight
        of angels the aviary of a wing-clipped heart for the cut flower,
fields, trees, earth, wrists, for the body torn,
                                    God.

Eden

I need an answer. There are no answers.
Nurses on nightshift—angels looking for wings,
Christ's night brides wandering the ward—
doctors—unbirthed miracles imbued with ambient light.
We were told to fear the monster
knitting fingers under the bed.
We didn't know it could be beautiful if you made it like fire.

I want to recall every detail:
how they turned your body the color of fall,
rotated sheets on your bed, unrolled them over your chest,
a bed of white roses in a half-moon glow,
a benediction of snow, machines flickering blue-red-blue-red,
wheezing like those floats we laughed at every 4th of July
standing on the corner with our shirts off,
radiant in the hot summer sun.

How they wheeled you off to radiology
rounding the corners of the hallways,
the way I remember growing up popping wheelies
with grocery carts, wobbling alongside aisles of soup cans, potato chips
spilling from our mouths onto the bleached linoleum,
men in coats as white as Mother's oleander,
scuffling their paper shoes like kites scaling windless summer air.

How they unfolded your body like a love letter,
emptied containers of needles,
beaks of syringes, pulled their fingers deep
into the glove's sunny sheen, humming show tunes,
adjusting shunts as though they were adjusting your tie,
bruises strung like violets up the light blue thread of your arms.

I want to remember the yank of curtains—
the halo of light surrounding your bed,
the smell of urine and Pine-sol, the temporary misshapen fragrance
of air, dispensers of evergreen, the shape, size, the jello's luminous glow,
rooms with windows you could look out of with only the lens of an eye,

everything upside down, carnivalized, the night in a dark blue suit,
pinstriped, sporting a crystal corsage, hooks on the shower curtain
skirting the metal rod, water that slid over your shoulders,
down the ravine of your back, water over a fall,
a rosary, the beaded bones, shadows passing under the door,
schools of fish, their silver-tipped tails glistening.

That the days sitting by your bed, the otherworldly sea fogged in,
whispers—breaths of birds, flowers, petals, hands
inside the womb of our mother, lucent stems—fingers still touching.
I didn't know it could be so beautiful—the swelling of flowers,
the bright metal walls of a crib, the bluish tint of the television,
a blessing, the dazzling scalpel.

I didn't understand the suddenness of what was happening:
lesions of rose, of periwinkle, clinging like vines to your face,
pulling like a weed at the thick red root of your heart,
dividing your organs cell by cell, liver, kidney,
how God could create heaven and earth,
the Garden flush with the brilliance of every living thing,
your body a perfect world for a perfect virus.

Better Angels I

Clothes plummeted onto floors, torn sacraments.
Everybody became a friend that died.
Who did I touch?
Desire tiptoed in from all directions.
Feverish roses bloomed on stained sheets.
Not me, thinking back as far as I could.
How many sheets spilled from my bed—
silent as snowfall, sunlight just beginning to rise
over the trail of an arm, a strand of hair?

Elegant bodies on the bed,
each cell an ornament filled with bright blood.
I danced and drank because I
didn't know what else to do,
two a.m., everyone out of breath, kissing the starved.
You could see through them, the dying
like stalks of celery shimmering in vodka.

Conversations occupied the past,
disinherited the future.
Everyone we ever touched, a mirror ball
that became the wild crane of a wrecking crew,
fragments of shattered glass,
a love garden diluted with ecstasy.

We became back stories of newspapers,
where a man lit himself on fire,
when no God would listen to him,
answer the terrible beating of his wings.

I saw bodies taken out of the sun,
heard doors closing in the hallways of Cedars, St. Mary's,
their corridors of grief, the color of breast milk.

Pills that made you sick.
Cures that made you die.
A decade of bruised gardenias grew.

I read unconsummated novels to pass the decade:
Werther at the fountains of unknown bliss,
Dostoevsky's hollow cheeks bounced off chandeliers.
We were all moving to Moscow, weren't we?
Ranevskaya kissing drapes,
the tender flesh of the walls, horses looking
back to find what they remembered
of themselves, the days fields, skies
imbedded stars, now darkening, now dying away,
laid down like a bandage as though skies over the city's
outskirts had wounded this earth.

Those long dark halls of the eighties—it was nothing.
Diana the hunted, the touch of her hand, a single
flame. And all the falling for decades, we, who
held flowers in our mouths, held photograph's,
held the dying, each someone who had gone before us,
before me.

I couldn't touch the morning, so I kissed the mirror.
I lay in bed, kissed the dark.
I couldn't touch the evening, so I kissed the mirror.

I kissed the mouths of telephone receivers.

I kissed the word goodbye.

I kissed caskets.

I kissed graves.

I kissed stillness.

I kissed everyone who had ever kissed me.

I kissed my brother's face, his dying.

I kissed the silence.

Better Angels II

Have you ever seen cherry trees in the spring?
How their stems grip frost,
wait for morning, a breath of air to open them?
That's how we felt,
like angels with our wings torn off.
This happened:
Mark, the Arc Angel, the funny one, was one of the first hit.
His laughter shook the air with radiant fists
from behind the bar where he worked until he was so thin
you could see through him,
shoulder blades sprouting from his body,
an oeuvre of olives, slices of lemon,
half-moon twist of lime,
jokes served open-faced on a white satin tongue.

His death terrified us all,
kept us from looking into mirrors, from touching,
from standing on scales.
We sat and drank Sundays, played pinball,
our t-shirts reflecting their bright magic,
dropping quarters into wells of blinking lights,
running up scores by pool tables,
the lamp swinging over our heads,
faces under interrogation as cue balls
broke into side pockets.

Nurses' mouths holed up. Reagan mute as a monster
until Nancy's hairdresser didn't show up for work one day.
Everywhere, everyone pressed against the dying bulb white air.
Think Louise Brooks after the gunshot, the still face.
We fell asleep in hospital waiting rooms,
watched the monochromatic brilliance of the moon,
smelled the odor of things shutting down,
soaps and chlorine.

We witnessed a generation changed in, changed out daily,
everything bought and sold, specific items burned, worn items.
Everyday someone was jumping.
It was like when the birds fell out of the sky one day,
entire flocks unexpectedly. But think months, years.
No one was listening, and we had become fewer and less,
voices like brooms over sidewalks.
Through the dying tone of this wind
we marched, even those who couldn't,
who had to be wheeled
out into the bright cloth of sunset,
ribbons pinned like claws to their chests,
little dead red things that fluttered in the breeze.
When they released my brother
from the hospital to go home and die,
a flurry of red had already covered his face,
rip through the fabric of his smile.
I thought: *if this happens to me.*

Elegy

"And yet we think the greatest pain's to die."
—John Keats, "On Death"

Keats writes in his garden
while my brother sleeps in the trees.

A gust of wind tousles his hair. His skin, white
in collapsing mist. I see my brother, the radiance
of sarcoma sprouting along his veins, rows
of violets in this same mist, the hospital corridor.
This must be how Keats
watched his brother John die, candle by the bed,
face flush, shadows stroking walls.
Only my shadows are on the ground moving over
the top of a hill as I stand, eye all the windows
of the sky open, the grass dry,
months pass, a week, another hour.

In the garden I yearn to govern
the way the bees govern—
honey-suckled, golden-rimmed,
improbable flight round
the probability of the flowered mouth,
the hemmed-in rose, the thorns,
wanting to make whole that which is not.

Awake on the hospital waiting room floor,
my body turns outward, my face marked
where my jacket's zipper pressed against
my cheek. The light from the hallway
passes over me, the dream gone, not dead, not dead,

my brother's IV infused with light
while all night his body burned.

Shirts flap on a clothesline.
Sleeves open and close,
another beauty, stark filled,
a coat of snow.
I don't remember the time of day he died.

> Over the lawn Christmas lights
> wired to the ground brightening
> my brother's crimson voltage.

Absentia

A truck on the road—
then nothing—
another car then nothing –
then something—
a voice slammed—
the sudden blow—of a door—
a light switch light—
keys on the table—
light through a window –
silence then stars –
nothing before the hand the hospital –
the door curtains pulled –
voices monitors asleep awake—
a network of oxygen molecules
then nothing after that—
immediately after the doctor—
your breath voices—
spoon his mouth then hands—
a tray of portable cures—
nurses circulating sterilized air—
a brother then nothing—
a fly speck—
useless nothing and nothing—
from nothing and why him—
and why not him—
why you and why—
not you why God—
and why not God—
and what difference
would feelings make
in an hour—in a day the ground—
turning then nothing—
then back the hour—

it takes out of you—
as far as you can see—
a town, a summer—
where silence escapes your ear—
year after year—
a turn on the highway—
light burrowing asphalt—
your brother—
a hole of a scream—
dead air—

coda i

They say the dying cannot see,
though their eyes flicker
as oxygen burns beneath their skin.
That the eyes are blown open temporarily
like a breeze through a curtain.

Twin I

I.

I had thought we'd said everything we needed to say
when you were in the hospital
and the nurses were running around

trying to figure
out how to make you more comfortable.
Would you like some more water?

But I continued to have entire conversations
with you in my head. Now, no one speaks.
You died of a virus no one knew the name of.

And when scientists found a name,
our parents declared that people like you
deserved to die.

No one would touch you.
No one from family went to your funeral.
Your body was burned.

II.

Trees lose leaves in winter. Every year birds return
to lusher resorts. No one thing ever leaves,
I tell myself, falls away completely.

When does it become unreasonable to cry?
I lay lilacs next to your headstone,
all of our family now gone, trace the letters

in your name, round out vowels
with my fingertips, shallowed out
beyond recognition to anyone but me.

Twin II

I was heard talking to myself,
compiling notes
of why it happened
when Hamlet wandered in looking for Ophelia,
who was looking in a mirror to find herself,
and I found myself peering
in that same mirror brushing the shower steam
aside as if I were still parting
clouds to find out what lay behind them,
you lying beside me in a nest in a tree,
an egg broken open, devoured,
your bed falling to the floor,
sheets descending, melting on the ground,
a network of light switches
in a house we no longer inhabit.
And there you are, standing beside me
holding my hand again,
a photo, the two of us, our hair anointed by light
healing our years apart.

Years later, when the two of us died,
I came to understand
why Ophelia was thought to have drowned herself
looking up as if to say *what if*,
wreathed in a flowerbed of watery asters,
mad with reason.
And you started talking again
when I wasn't looking for you
in a garden of the same name,
my hand turning the soil over
and over as if I might find you there.
That was then. And afterward,
this is now, running my fingers

through my hair as if it were your eyes
staring back at me,
as if it were your body of flowers,
your mouth open,
your hair tying up loose ends of water.

Twin III

Where are you?
You were supposed to meet me
at the bar a half hour ago.
I saved a seat for you,
ordered you a drink,
appetizers from that skinny waitress.
Since you hadn't shown up,
I thought maybe the clock stopped.
If I can't depend on you,
who can I depend on?
We've been together for so long.
Say, do you remember
that summer at camp
we got so sunburned
we had to sleep naked on the sheets,
all the windows open,
the moon on our legs?
Love you, you said, looking out the window.
Neither of us could sleep
for all the stars.
Remember walking to school?
Jumping the railroad tracks?
I thought I lost you in those fields
behind the house.
The first time I felt terror.

Listen to me.
I noticed you were
in the shower with me this morning
while I cried, washed my hair,
brushed my teeth.
I thought those were your hands.
I could sure use another drink

right about now.
A double martini.
I like the shape of the glass,
like a big surprise.
It would be funny if.
Sorry I ate all the chicken wings.
What did you say you wanted
for our birthday?

Maybe I should lay off the drinks.

Our hands join time.
We dream swimming the same rivers.
Two contours of one shadow play
against the wall. Your face returns.

I'm starting to think you're alive.

Twin IV

> "Love consists in this: that two solitudes
> protect and touch and greet one another."
> —Rainer Maria Rilke

1.

In the woods, birds lift the sky.
My eyes follow them past the trees,
through the swarm of sunlight,
until hours disappear.
Rilke confesses he can see through a bough
the emptiness of a rainy day.
I can't see past yesterday.
The mention of rain appears later in the poem.
Was it in winter you died?
Was it summerless?
The sun-drenched woods smell like new hours,
a handful of silences.
April's what I remember,
April's the heart of the matter.
The windows to your room open.
I look up and can't see your face through the curtains.
I hear a storm gather, a hammering.
Now birds gather under the backyard tree.
No larks this time, but your body moving.
This is where my wounds start, memory begins.
I try to capture the act of forgetting.
The perfectly drawn line from one end of my life
to the other,
my breath, in the cold, three steps ahead.
It will get to where I'm going before I do.
It will touch you.
Clouds separate behind me, so that I might look back
and see what I've done with my life.
In the distance, I see you, still as the world never is.

2.

I dismiss whatever I think I am.
What I need is to free myself from what I'm accustomed to.
the bureau, the bed, the floor.
A hospital sheet flung
out the window becomes a cloud.
This poem, a thimbleful of rain,
grandmother holding a parcel behind her back.
It isn't always what I think it is,
this room, this life.
The word "death" swells like heat.
My eyes are the edge of me.
I've followed them, hoping they will find meaning.
Here is where the idea of a tree blooms –
in this tree, the entire world.
No one hears the bruising of apples
that fall from night.
In the morning,
I've learned to cradle them gently.

3.

In my mind I'm an old man saying,
or as Rilke says, "*ein altes Sprichwort.*"
When I see you, it can be in a grove
where a great storm wraps around you.
When you leave, sound empties.
A curved scream, you arrive—
our childhood, a coloring.
Our past makes small but vital appearances.
I hold it in my hand.
In prayer, a cathedral rises.
I become *ein altes Sprichwort.*
You are what I want.
Sometimes I feel love this way.
Sometimes it is the hesitation that the breath broods.
Hiding, swept from corners.
I crave what I cannot have, rust in shade.
Across from me, a knife.
I take an apple and slice it.
Aren't both sides of light
one and the same?
What holds them together?
The body has its own vision of the heart.
One mirrors the other,
as this apple remains perfect and separate.
There is an argument to be made here.
You never left but are.

Social Distancing

Love the sinner, not the sin, my mother said,
my hands folded in front of me, praying.
The pastor would not bury my brother.
His virus was not tolerated by neighbors.
At the time, they called my brother an abomination.
Prayers filled the church, forgiving him his sins.
You shall not lie with a male
as one lies with a female; it is an abomination,
sunlight hammering windows,
Jesus holding shards of glass.

I fly out the windows, sit in a tree.
A God Bird is waiting for me.
Go back inside, it tells me.
Where am I safe? I ask him.
I wake up crying,
my blanket dropped to the floor.
A clock tells me I'm dreaming.
I walk around the room
go to a window, look out,
up until morning
searching for god birds
holding my dead brother's hand.

Ingress

Nothing stops him from opening
my mouth, entering quiet rooms
of my body, scent of his skin,

lips red as camellias.
If I speak his name no difference.
He always whispers in my ear.

I take him in, this grief.
He runs his fingers through the thickening
shadows of my hair.

Sometimes my food tastes of him
as a word enters my mouth.
He salts my tongue in the dark.

I see him only when I've stopped
looking. Like countless lanterns
through my ribs, up the long

ladder of my spine. He drifts
through the chambers of my heart.
Brilliant, this grief never dims.

I can't look at him directly
no more than I can stare
into the face of the sun.

Knees, hips, shoulders, arms.
I am back to him on all fours,
a moon on water.

I lift his body. He lifts mine.
My wrists swell. You can read

when something reminds it
of what it once was, how an arm
once fell. Sometimes, I just

want to be recognized.
He comes to help me remember,
everything about you that was alive.

Evolution

I.

I'm rooted to this chair, reading this book,
facing my reflection in the window where I
see you, still, waiting for me to enter, your
hand, the yellow curtain pulled to one side,
just two rooms, no mirrors.

It's four in the morning.
I want to touch you so you know
I know you're still alive.

When you disappear you forget everything, become
a flower, a field, wind, a heat blazing forever,
a paved road, a stop sign, a scrap of an exchange,
a lost word, a photograph, a slap on the wrist,
a broken chime, that child under the table tying
his shoelaces.

Don't blame my hands, my mouth. They're
waiting for the flip of a switch, bright, bright
as a kitchen.

I found an abalone shell, ran my finger
over the broken edge and thought of my
older brother, the war, his leg shot off, hemorrhaging
like an ocean. I was seven years old when
he took me to the beach and nearly let me drive
into the water, the birds   flying over us,
loud as helicopters.

Stars. Exhibitionists.

I heard him whistling last night, looking up at
stars as if he'd just seen a gallery of faces—brothers,
aunts, uncles, nieces, wives that watch him sweep floors,
empty trashcans, scrub toilets, fold dinner napkins,
close curtains, the curtains that keep sunlight from entering
the church at night, balancing the moon on the tip of his tongue.

I'm alone. I hear a boy laugh, see him point his finger,
a book, pages falling, falling.

                    How beautiful my mother is: Why would
                    she do this to me? I loved her so much that day
                    because I knew I would hate her for life,
                    that I would always hear her pulling
                    out of the driveway and never, ever coming back.
                    Not the same way. Not the same way.

The lawnmower torturing the grass,
the sprinkler caressing it.

                    I hear her walking, spreading the carpet
                    thin, opening the door to my bedroom,
                    kicking it closed. Then autumn:
                    leaves shuddering, the ground taking them
                    in, footprints everywhere. Why do you
                    hate me?

What makes a childhood's death
the buried body of a song?

                    Did I mention the photograph, the guy to the right of
                    those three who was her Harry,
                    the one who died. Oh sweet small
                    orchard of pears, apples spinning,
                    browning through the years, smiling,

full of seed, dust around the corners
of their mouths where there was a shade
of red once, the aftertaste of rain.

As deep as any memory —
the flowing, the river, that sort of paradise
that wind carries, that windows
open to, and doors cut from a tree in that
same paradise, affirming, confessing.

Dip your feet into the ocean, now blue, now
green, now sapphire.

II.

He leaned into her. She kissed him on the forehead.
See how light breaks branches.
See how the stars give way.

Sometimes I wonder what it would feel like
to walk upside down and what a postman
might look like delivering mail, letters—
birds of our own making.

I feel the sky, hear my mother whisper.
A grasshopper sputters.

These hours of loneliness.

The Romans wrote of seasons then captured
them in stone, nothing but living then,
and planning one's survival.
Then they burned their city down.

The way a mother carries her child
after a long day, how her body bends,
the wind stirring.

I want to be something
I swore I would never forget,
that boy in the field by Winslow.
He takes me to where I'm going.

I smell her hair.
I still smell her hair.

 I ripped her letter to shreds.

And I think who cares as I look up the road at that new
batch of roses flooding the air, roots crawling over bones.

I am a beginner in this world.

Anniversary

Trees remember dying, each fall losing leaves, the bundled light.
The sun shines through them and rain colors the branches dark as rivers.

Swallows abandon them for warmer weather.
Barren, nothing sings to them in their warded state.

Then spring arrives and everything that once was blooms again,
the grass as though it'd never left, old hat, sky in hand, all desire.

Year after year what is broken is restored.
Unaccountable deaths. Unaccountable births.

And just when I think I'm beginning to understand the circular motion of birds
and the rings of trees, the trunks split, the opening wood,

and the unhappiness I feel, the night-grief and all the days remembering
your body in the doorway and how your laugh tilted the frame of your interior.

I remember the year of your dying, your footprints in the snow
like the hooves of elk and how simple your death seemed to me at the time

when I could not see clearly as when the body moves without thinking,
and could not imagine death as something wonderful.

I listened to the wind blowing through the empty trees,
remember the body's dying as that of the tree, the lessening, the becoming.

Each morning our bed sheets darken. Shadows of tree limbs turn in the light,
the way light in rivers turn at certain times of the day never touching bottom

and everything that once was is again, only rising, and the trees fill again with light,
then color arrives before I know it, the copper maple, the oak, the burning red leaves

of the sycamore. I hear the sound of wood, the rings split, the dusk behind you.

Remnants

An unoccupied birdhouse, an empty hummingbird feeder,
a slow tempered sun bears down over the fields
like light bearing down over an ocean before it turns

black, fat and fathomless. You step into
this empty field, feel stones rock the bottoms
of your shoes as you grind a path you've been grinding

for years. For argument's sake you call it life.
You could die in silence and lie in the grass
for months before anyone would find you,

anyone of family, friend , stranger, a few curious birds,
lying alone with ants crawling around your ankles.
But not to worry because back in the ground

you'll go after a good flood like the Baptists teach,
the deluge that wipes away
any regret you ever had in your life for not starting something

you wanted to start but forgot somehow—
forgot why you were brought here in the first place
and who it was you were supposed to please

because in your mind you had everything
you ever needed to go as far as you wanted to go
before the virtuous and righteous Reverend Michaels

taught you the knowledge of sin from the age of five.
Off you went, peddling your encyclopedia of God,
selling knowledge of afterlives, heaven, hell,

God's essence breathing down your neck,
sopping your armpits, the length of your spine,
through all those teenage years making out

in the backseat of your family Chrysler,
slipping fingers inside underwear
thinking god almighty this feels good

getting lost in the brightness of something so wonderful
it only came to you in dreams—
a remembering that came to you late in life

when you took a walk one day in October
to get the mail, the newspaper you never had any use for in the first place,

all the guilt and sins of the world rolled up in the Virginia Sentinel
where crimes committed by locals are posted,
misdemeanors for swearing, public impairment, arraignments,

a thin-skinned sin of a newspaper not worthy of the blue sky
falling around you, the windows of your house filled,
birds rattling the dead wind of a summer evening with their music,

clouds opening and closing the same doors you wanted to walk through,
looking up at them with a hole in your heart—
all those years you thought the two plastic birds on your grandparents

front lawn were not ducks but geese, their long slim necks pruning the sunlight;
discovered the green frog frosted with mold was really a turtle,
and the stubble of wood that looked like a chair was not a chair at all

but a tree charred by lightning to a fraction of what it was,
cut down as it reached for a higher blue, a kinder weather,
you still rooted, hands in pockets digging to find something

you lost years ago and will never find again.
Sit down on the charred tree.

You won't be survived by anyone.

coda ii

Here love is audible.
They brought me here, those still remembered
Sunlight is ransacked.
My hands are in my pockets.
My feet press down on the grass.
My shadow lies here, here, here—
here is my head,
arms, legs,
my root crown,
my body stem.

How Did I Come Here?

I lie awake in the history of a small house
on a small acreage that opens a small window
where I have never lived.
All that surrounds these hills moves toward me.
It's summer, cloudless.
I lie on the grass like a stone,
live in the sky's wakefulness,
in the quickness of hummingbirds,
their bright-shelled delving.
I live in the fields, in the moisture's temperament.
I break in the heat.
The pond in back of the house is the mirror
I use to travel backward in time. I live here,
where the waters of childhood linger,
flex against the shallows,
the length of a shoe.
Roads spin gravel and dust.
Always someone arrives from miles away.
Always someone arrives from miles away.
Wild blackberries fingerprint my arrival.
I pick them through a fence that stings me.
Theirs is a sweetness I've never tasted,
a bitterness that never leaves my tongue
Buzzards sway like door hinges, pick the ground.
What came before? I do not know.
Rain arrives after heat drinks.
Ground diets on bone and weather.
What it refuses lies like armor.
I cannot make this more than it is:
my shirt parceled beneath the limbs of a tree,
my mother in the kitchen.

Walking Backward

1.

Daylight seeps through curtains, searches for landings,
photographs—the storytelling of hats, hairstyles,
shirts, dresses, documentation of hemlines.
A hand carved chair reclines in the corner
where my grandfather sat, reading the *Evening Star,*
his face, the water of his eyes
through rusted skin, a biography of Junes through late August.
He falls asleep in that chair one summer, never wakes.

Voices of the missing rise everywhere.
As I turn the corner, I see two empty chairs at the end
of the road facing west. In one of them I see my father.
In the other, my mother sits gazing over long distances.
He is running his finger over her wrist.
She is flattening apples stitched inside the creases of her apron.
Their hands -gray and mottled leaves,
their expressions, illegible script.

They say the farther the distance from the object
blocking the light to the surface of projection,
the larger the silhouette. When I witness them now,
they are larger than I have ever known.
I walk around to the back of the house, lose my reflection
in my bedroom window, a face within unnumbered faces.
A face that pulls me toward it, but never grants entry.

A house stitched by time and ancestral industry.
Floorboards expand, nails give.
Lightbulbs with questionable circuitry flicker.
The bannister glides alongside the staircase.
A hand-worn arm, it secures the flight of family—
arrivals, departures, semi- annual returns.

Days are long, wide-open vowels.
You could swing through them—
they are that wide. Fields, we all have them,
dark spines in fall, translucent spires
in spring, fields of small worlds, universes, heavens.
Livings are made here, though at times summer
seems to make the land unlivable
for the sun's bruising.

2.

The land's accompaniment: suites of bird's nests—
northern pintail, blue-winged teal.
Wild carrot wed the front yard fence.
Foxglove, loosestrife conversed by the well.
In the spring, butterfly weed bloomed,
procured the annual return of the rusted
patch bumblebee, the white admiral.
Everywhere, the ground reminds me of what it can bear.

A thermometer anchored on the back porch door
registers the size of the weather—
heat, length, duration, its gradual expansion
to include probabilities of moisture,
hazards of gnats, water striders, habitats of land
that have been schooled in genealogy,
in the fluctuating roles of a Midwestern upbringing.
You might catch a breeze or two stalled around the edges,

a balm from the tireless drafts of seasonal jays,
thrashers airing out their rooms at the box elder.
Already July's summer has begun to pummel the lawn,
filter through the spectacles of myrtles.
Dust motes disband inside bright yellow sheets.

3.

It makes good company.
The barn holds its birthplace near the well.
Light breaks through a crack in the window, a lens
like that of a film projector in an old movie theatre
that widens, searches for a wall on which to tell my story.
Every day, something inside it grows from the dark—a word,
a laugh that can run a ring around you as old as the trees.
A church bell: a swarm of bees pilots the air and its silence.

If I close my eyes, I see Mrs. Applegate
and the Petersons who lived two miles down the road, next door.
Their son Billy was killed in the war. Mrs. Peterson got a medal
and a flag. He got a write-up in the local Sunday paper.
Billy and I grew up together, side by side, sailing our oceans,
writing our chapters. What I knew of love I learned from him.
Thirty years. I still feel his absence beside me.

You can see where the wallpaper is still beautiful, still a field.
I am happy to be home where nothing falls away completely,
where things remain, where golden-asters tip their crowns,
white admirals marshal and Queen Anne lift their veils.
Early evening's simmering this land that binds life
to death, their escapes, the sun to the innermost darkness
of the trees, to the wind quietly rocking. The Midwest
never lets go, the leave's cymbals, the copper-red sky
thick as the blood that runs through me
as I sit and look out the window, wonder
how I came to be in the world, the slight flight
of a firefly, tying its night-string to one of a trillion, trillion stars.

Leviticus

Cousin Billy lights a cigarette,
cups the flame in front of his mouth.
Don't tell Janet.
She doesn't know I smoke.
He takes a drag.
She'd kill me if she knew.
Billy is filled with minor disturbances.

I'm sorry about yesterday.
We don't care what you are.
We've all got our sins he says,
and stands tongue-tied. It seems like forever.
This type of silence never marries.

Billy examines the Johnson grass by the porch.
It'll kill everything if you let it.
Better start bush hogging, otherwise.
He flicks his cigarette and goes indoors.
Don't tell Janet 'bout the bourbon neither.
The screen door slams shut.
An hour's heat chases after him.

Janet approaches me from the other side of the yard.
We're sorry about what the minister said yesterday.
You know Billy and I don't feel that way.
Janet's vowels are long and drawn and sweet.
Janet does not suffer minor disturbances.
Complications do not rifle her.

She sits down, folds the hem of her dress over her knees.
No one cares who's gay, but why do they
always have to rub it in our faces, she asks.
It's their choice. Her vowels: long, drawn, sweet.

She tells me that she loves me because I am family.
It's the way we are here honey, forgiving.
Come inside before dinner gets cold!

You don't waste time chatting in the Midwest.
At dinner, you learn to pass the plates
before the gravy begins to settle
and conversations turn to silence.
You learn just how close to family
you're ever going to be.

Myrtles cast shadows over the lawn.
I pick up a stone, roll it in my hand,
throw it as hard as I can,
out of my sight.

Goddam hard as I can.

Memorial with Liminal Space

for my cousin David

Part tractor, trailer
Semi-conductor
Toolbox, heart
Hands a part
Of something larger
Then the sum of his parts

Part country, field
House, table, chair
Window, landing
The ladder that parts air
A mountain
Shoulders three feet apart
Eyes: part river, lake
Closed off, open
The part that runs out to sea

His heart stopped
From six feet up,
A ladder apart from the sky
Dropped like a wrench
You could see where he fell,
His mother said.
You could hear him try to get air

That part of the ground
Part of his heart
Stopped
Now part of the earth
Grown apart from the sky
Part of the land he grew up in
Part root, water, stone.
I still see him, his mother said.
Uprooted from ground. Not dead.

Before the Wedding

Early morning, the two of us up.
I slip downstairs to the bathroom.
Floorboards creak. They are just getting to know me.
In the kitchen, June turns the coffee pot on.
Fits of steam gurgle, a hospital of newborns.
I open the newspaper, wander up
and down petite plumbed columns, pages
whisper, leaves swept up by a broom.
June enters with two coffee mugs.
We warm our hands around them.
I have something I want to show you she says.
She unbuttons her nightgown.
The collar falls open like wings, perhaps petals.
Perfume escapes into the room.
This is where the doctors cut me open, she says.
Glue dilates in the extractions.
A compound of adhesive keeps her skin from tearing.
The scarring—a drowned-out purple-violet,
as if torn open by rain,
rises from breastbone to breastbone.
I had the doctor cut them both off, she says.
Calm sustains her equanimity and mine.
She's eighty-four, my mother's sister.
I have come for her wedding tomorrow.
Western shadows lean away from daylight.
Eastern bluebirds pick up their squabbles.
She buttons her blouse, now petals, now closed.

Solitary Confinement

> "The world is governed by chance. Randomness stalks us every day of our live."
>
> —Paul Auster

A dog tells me where I cannot go. There are fences everywhere, no one else for what seems miles.

Hummingbirds pillage the groundcover. Purple loosestrife gain, spring hoverfly hold
to what breezes they can, foxglove, wild carrot root like tossed bridal gowns.

The house to my left is the house where I lived. A tricycle disintegrates where the heat got to it.

A swing emptied over the lawn, a mother's voice in the kitchen, a father's boots
dropped to the floor. An open window turns the temperature out.

Beyond the house a field where my brother and I hid, a yellow field, moon-burned, where we hunted
        crickets,
                held ice-colored mice, bright as stars.

The rusted barrel where I hid my brother's tennis shoes has a tear where the weather's been.
A branch on the ground leans toward it. Nothing is too dark to be lived in.
                    Ask the Owl, my brother said.
                    Silence never leaves the throat entirely.

White blooms, everywhere on the tips of trees, open moonlight.

The barn has a tin roof the rain clawed, empty of everything but summer moods. I hear the stream behind our
house, fish withdraw between green-husked stones. Salmon, trout, drag the water.

The moon relinquishes the past. Our feet languish at the water's edge.

The church bell rusts. Still, it has a lever to be pulled, sound to open.

The bright ballast of the front yard trees echoes the wind and the arms that swung from them,
                my brother's laughter as round
                as the mouth of a tire stars fill.

Rubbed leaves split underfoot, trumpet the soil. Where there were feet, there's no more color.

Someone is heard singing in a kitchen of baked bread. I remember all the words,
the skywardness through the curtains, the faint whistling drawing circles with its pitch,

what a mother sounds like, a father, an untethering, a thread, the muddy constellation of a shoe.

There's no end to the journey.

I mean such things as this: the way a fish glances toward sky, asters of eyes, sweet moss remains.

Hymn

The Midwest settles into a blue temperature.
The landscape darkens and I am inside it.
I look out as the last of day's light diminishes.
Hills and seamless grasses merge.
Where one field ends another begins.
Queen Anne reign expanded kingdoms.
Clouds disperse. Early stars fill the dark.
Here evenings even everything they touch.

Congregations of bluebirds dilate branches of Myrtle,
Jacaranda, accompany their color,
the afternoon's last breezes owed to these birds,
to their seasonal carpentries,
to the upward sweep of their hymns.
Tomorrow, I will go home.
My visit, long and long enough.

I wonder a lot about the love of family, its flight,
what photographs I take with me,
brochures I leave behind.
Where someone is dead, someone is alive.
I don't know what I learn about parents
except what I don't.
Conversations of silence surround the evening meal,
consist of a tap on the knee under the dining room table.
Perhaps, seems, maybes, ifs scale our family tree.
What's said has already been said thousand-fold.

The older I become the more I imitate my father.
Seems he and I've been rowing for generations.
Each year I blow out birthday wishes.
Newspaper clippings folded inside the family bible
record our family's gradual decline.
I've learned that goodbyes arrive in
groups of twos and threes,

that no one leaves alone.

Retakes

"Life was created in the valleys. It blew up into the hills on the old terrors, the old lusts, the old despairs. That's why you must walk up the hills so you can ride down."
—William Faulkner, *As I Lay Dying*

1.

Fields bend in wind.
Soon hay will have to go under.
I lie on grass like a stone, live
in the sky's wakefulness,
leaves that spin ornaments.
A hummingbird's path between
branches, brightens. Finches
chatter in nests of little dark rooms.
Aunt June calls from the kitchen.
Dinner is on the table- squash,
potatoes. "We're having pork chops tonight.
Come inside before the mosquitoes get you."
She's a tall woman with hair as bright
as milk and ankles the size of
small cantaloupes. She's my mother's only sister
and hugs me as if I were her own,
the mother I never knew,
whose photo I keep inside my wallet,
tucked away like an heirloom.

2.

I live in moisture's temperament.
My body lies still in dampening grass.
I look toward fields that will soon
need to go under,
already bent with seed
for next year's crop.

I hear finches chattering in trees.
They have found little rooms of darkness
between branches to build nests.
A sudden wind scatters the heat.
Aunt June hollers from the porch.
Harry and my other cousins are coming
up the road. Here you can hear someone
arrive from miles away.
In the summer, you can hear dust rise.
I get up on my elbows,
pick up a small stone and pitch it
toward the pond. The water, startled at first,
quickly calms.

3.

Aunt June is a big woman
with a hive of white hair
and ankles the size of grapefruits.
She was a beauty once. Still is.
She has the tenderness of someone
damaged, but not scarred.
She holds me as if I were hers.
I don't remember my mother
holding me, or even what she
looked like. Outside, I lie on grass
like stone, live in the moistures
temperament. All that dwells in
these hills swims toward me.
Fields bend in wind.
Soon they will need to go under,
the seeds planted in late fall
before the ground swells with frost.
I hear a finch building her nest.
She is fastidious, darting between
the branches, leaves spinning like ornaments.
I live in a silence, what being inside a
breath must feel like,
or the fold of a hand.

4.

I hear dust rise, pebbles grind.
Someone is coming up the road
to visit the Clemmons'.
I lie on grass and live
in the day's wakefulness.
A finch seems to be arguing.
She chatters as she moves
from limb to limb and
drapes of leaves shuffle.
She's furnishing her nest
in rooms of shade,
and someone turned
the sprinkler on.
I live here where hills
swim toward me,
where grass bends
and moisture clings to my clothes,
anchors me to ground.
Aunt June said it was the hottest
day on record. This is my first day here.
I arrived from miles away.
Already the sky is familiar.

5.

It will stay. It has never left.
My mother's voice embroidering the trees,
in the falling. I lie on my
back, live in the sky's wakefulness,
the hummingbirds delving,
the bright shell. Aunt June is
in the kitchen mixing dough
for biscuits tonight. I can hear
cabinets open and close
like instruments. All that lives

in these hills swims toward me.
Like tender lapping of voices.
I hear them speaking. A finch
builds its nest in the eaves.
I hear its heart beating.
The wind never leaves.
The fields with their backs
bent, seeds beginning
like a child's beginning,
almost intelligible, an engrained voice
joining what I know to what
I have never known.
I hear chattering in a tree.
Too hot, the finch seems to be saying.
No places to build nests.
No small spaces a mother might consider.

6.

There is more light than these trees
know what to do with. A warm
breeze jostles the leaves.
They spin like coin.
I live in the moisture's temperament.
Blades of grass stick
to my shirtsleeves.
Soon, fireflies will appear,
leave their extinguished bodies
on the ground. June told me
when she was a little girl,
she and my mother used to take
the fireflies and stick them
to their foreheads
then run around
the backside of the house
to the pond and throw them,
watch water split into galaxies.

7.

I arrive at a place
that I have never left,
like childhood,
as familiar as my breath.
I lie on the grass like a stone.
I hear my mother's voice in these trees.
All that lives in these hills
swims towards me.
I live in the sky's
wakefulness, in the hummingbird's
bright-shelled delving.
In the pond behind the house, I live,
a place where I witness myself becoming.
I live in the moisture's temperament.
My shirtsleeves stick to grass.
There are acres and acres
of grain to be harvested.
Their stalks bend in heat.
Soon they will go under.
Aunt June says that you must wait
until fall, that you can't plant
anything around here too soon
or it will die before it ever has a chance.

8.

Always someone or something
arrives from what seems miles away,
like a memory, something folded
in trees, in the hummingbird's
bright delving, a wakefulness that
cannot be described, except that
it lives. I lie on grass
like stone. All in these hills that

surround the house swim towards me.
Fields bend, steeled with grain.
Soon they will have to go under.
I hear combines in the distance.
I hear the dust rise. A nest of gnats
swirls around my face. I brush
them away but it's like brushing fog.
The pond in the back is my mother's coat.
I hear Aunt June inside the house.
She is my mother's only sister
and hugs me as if I were her own,
my mother whom I never knew,
whose photo I keep inside my wallet
tucked away like an heirloom.

9.

I watch as each day moves forward
on its own, my arms outstretched
to what is new but what feels as
familiar as my own breath.
At dinner, conversations rise like steam
from the corn, from the bowl
of mashed potatoes, the garden squash.
My cousins Bobby, Butch, and Jim
pass plates, ladle gravy.
Aunt June says the Clemmons' lost a cow.
"A dead cow has to be dragged
off the field so other cows
don't see it", she says to me.
"It frightens them, the sight
of one of their own dying in the field.
Anyway, the heat carries the smell for days."
"It's been over one hundred degrees
for two weeks, longest on record.
Maybe that's what killed her," I say.

Bobby looks at me.
Bobby has irises the color of chipped ice.
June blots her lipstick.
The others at the table
grab their forks, take on
the last few ham slices,
what's left of the dinner rolls.
I live here, inside everything, at once,
these dinner conversations, rinsing the dishes,
in the veined light trickle.

10.

It's here I see myself becoming
the present and the presence joined.
Yesterday, I picked wild strawberries,
picked them through a fence that stung.
I put them in my mouth.
I had never tasted such sweetness,
felt such bitterness leave my tongue.
There's permanence here, a steady rhythm.
It's as if the sky held my absence,
as if the clouds were my mother's apron,
and the loose strings, branches
writing her name every
morning over the pond.
I look out over the front lawn,
at leaves unraveling,
plastic geese molting,
the tree stump carved into a chair,
the stone rabbit in the garden
with its one bandaged ear.
I live in the day's gossip,
in the breathless phrases of wind
swiveling through the laundry,
inside what has come
to me so late in life.

Hummingbirds are ornaments.
Aunt June, Bobby, Jim, the Clemmons' cow,
fireflies falling like stars,
each leaving a sentence of light.
My mother's voice burns in the grass.
In the afternoons, I walk
with nowhere to go.
I have found few answers, watching
clouds empty, the dusk,
and the early stars approach.
Sometimes at night,
I dream I see my mother.
She walks toward me from a great distance.
She holds her palms out like empty spoons.
And I having nothing I want to give her.
The roads grind pebbles and dust.
Always someone arrives from miles away.
Always someone arrives from miles away.

No Use for Language Spoken Everywhere

I.

You're sitting on the porch, Sunday, same as an hour before, long after the morning rain and the drainpipe next to me remembering sunlight and cloud's opening, dropping consonants, exploding vowels. Weren't you here this morning trying to figure things out, looking for words when the whole sky turned over on itself, how it reminded you of Asters and how they reminded you that there are things
to do with time and that weather on your hands.

You try to open your hands, spread your fingers as if they were trying to figure out bees circling. When did it happen, where were you and what year was it that one of your brothers died, the other two brothers before. What summer was it, what was the day and when exactly? How quiet's stubbornness reminds you of a particular time and particular hour when what you wanted to do was think and all that was required was that you listen.

There's been a lot of news about the hippocampus, how it stores information and root causes. How it catalogs incidences, aftermaths finding their way back to you as you do the dishes, fold laundry, toss clothes back into shape.

That day at the office or standing at the kitchen counter mashing potatoes, turning the burners on. Was it something important you were supposed to remember about rain, dampness, cold? Weren't the yellow tails trying to tell you something about nests and the overtures of family?

Then God again, scrubbing the clouds, clearing the air and all the blue rising. There it is again, the parting, the opening, the falling through, the starting over. Less time between sounds now, those drops. Water silenced and you right back where you started, washed away and taking in the sky head on. That talking you wanted to let go of, hand over your mouth, covering your face, recording it all.

II.

It's that kind of weather after an October storm, bluer than sky knows what to do with, more trees filled with light, more feverish sun, more silence, more waking, less sleeping, sounds coming back as if they are not quite sure where the steady grass is, what trees are safe, ants moving across the sunlit porch. It's the small gestures that get you, a breeze turning a corner, holding, letting go, holding again, becoming a hand

that reminds you of someone you once loved, that moved over your chest, muscles, blood, heart, moved in and out of your mind, filling holes, those empty buckets you left hoping someone other than yourself would fill. You tell yourself love happens that way, as a storm of finches flies by, turning the light over and over again and no one for miles, for days. Rain gone leaving you with

nothing but heart and mind turning toward one another, then outward toward a bluer sky. What it was before the rain came and erased everything as if it and you never existed. Before the loosening of crickets over the lawn, fireflies igniting and reigniting, your Aunt June in the house, lying on the sofa having already taken her teeth out, having bitten off a good chunk of ninety-two years, television on, watching old
westerns. What was good and bad drifting though her living room, windows hanging on for a couple more turns of light before they go black.

You can't love her *more* or *less*, you tell yourself. You can't save her. You can't save yourself. You can't save anyone or anything. Not even the light.

III.

Aunt June had two breasts removed six months ago. Now she's singing like a lark, running around town doing the grocery shopping, banking, picking up the dry cleaning, the blue of her eyes a sky holding the world together in what must have been God's year off. *If you don't know where love is, go out and find it at the kitchen sink.*

This year she tells you that she gets dizzy sometimes, that it springs up out of no-where. She shows you her hand, where she fell, where the bone broke and tried to push through her wrist, leaving her fingers curled upward as if they were trying to hold on.

There are two more headstones at the family graveyard than the last time you were here, two more holes dug, two more bodies that the world got tired of. You think you see yourself there, at the end of the third row, stone polished, your name freshly engraved, telling you that there's more to learn from dying than living. You listen to the ground after a rain pulling the sunlight with it, pull it down by the hand, your roots

pulled with it, pulled in every direction, then perhaps grass, flowers growing, something of yourself you want the world to remember. If you're lucky, a swarm of finches. The neighbor's horse is staring at you as if to tell you I told you so. The cows have known what's been coming for years. The things you think about after a rain, or not. Maybe you're here for no other reason than to, once a year, sit on a bench and write it

down, to look up now and then and listen to the living, then back again to the end and the still dying. The thought of someone you love in the house, the brightness of June's skin when it turns to summer, her bulb-white hair. Don't move. You don't want to ruin this, the early moon, the earlier stars. *Wherever you are you've already been heard.*

IV.

She is more like a bird, you think, singing in the morning, waking the trees up, flying over the lawn, as if pulling the sheets over the bed, taut at the corners, making day up from night. It's how she rearranges things, the way birds rearrange nests, drawing the damp out of them, drawing in sunlight, the day

rising and falling, and all the silence folded inside every living thing, the lacewing, the monarch, what it does when it has something to say. It's the silence in her eyes, silence she sees with, shakes by the shoulders, waking into the next hour. We're all planning our demise. Listen:

I'm getting my hair done today. It's the only time Marietta can take me. Will you drive me there and what is all this wood on the porch and those darn spiders and I love this house, this land. It's as if God touched it. Who would ever want to leave?

It's been a year since my last visit. Is it possible that the clouds are where they were last year and that the trees have the same leaves, the same shape folded over, the tree behind the house pointed upward like a spear? The grass looks the same. It spreads over the yard down the slopes, tucked in at the corners of the house, rubbed smooth from the heat and last night's rain, the hand of God. And there's that view

again, the curve of the hill before you get to the main road, a slope like a shoulder, arms reaching as far as the road will take them. And the hand like those trees reaching where there's still light to be had. I want to make noise here before I get lost. I want to walk in the graveyard, trace the letters of the names of those

that came before me, having come here one day out of a week out of a month running my fingers over headstones, tracing family that were not there the last time I came to visit a woman who came to find something of herself in the silence, a woman standing behind the screen door looking out at the land she chose never to leave, that chose never to leave her.

coda iii

No ordinary thing the bowl, the cup,
the glass you hold to your lips, the knife,
the fork, the spoon you lick, the apple
you slice, the orange you peel, the scent,
its wave, the taste of living.

Inbox

Trash

Trash

Save the one from your mother.

Trash

Trash

Trash

Save the one from your brother. The last one.

Save the one from your brother that you mean to go see.

The one from two years ago.

Archive all the e-mails from your grandmother.

She doesn't remember who you are. Remind yourself.

Trash

Trash

Save the e-mail from your high school teacher. She's still singing in your head.

Archive the last e-mails from yourself to your doctors and all the things

that can hurt your kidneys.

There are more prescriptions to be filled.

Save all the e-mails from your insurance company. Someone

is always coming back for you.

Trash

Trash

Trash

Save the one from that friend you never got back to. You still mean to.

Save the one from your Aunt in Virginia. She'll be ninety this year.

She's the only one who knew your mother. You want to see her this year.

There's a virus going around.

Save the one from your broker. There's a virus going around.

Trash e-mails from old friends that you will never read again.

That remind you of things that you should have done.

That remind you that time is running out.

That you didn't get where you wanted to be.

Save the one from yourself to yourself to remind yourself.

Trash old photos.

Trash all the attachments to the lake: the house, all the summers, fall.
Trash the incoming from unidentified senders. They want to sell you something
you don't need until you think you need it.
Save the one from your lover who has trouble breathing. Save that sound.
Save the hours between you. Save the fight from last night.
Save the empty space between, the last syllable.
Save the photo of the two of you on the lake. The cold blowing through.
The wind moving you over the water. The sun bouncing back from the water.
Save the way it touched you.
Save the way it touches you still.
Archive the mountains. The snow.
Save the boarding pass. Save the hard copy.
Save the last hour in the hospital room.
Save him smiling in the bed like he smiled at the lake.
Save every e-mail he ever sent you
to remind you of something you needed to do but forgot to.
Start over. Trash all.
Delete unread messages.
Trash all the drafts.
You still hear him.

Anatomy

Our bodies turn, a hip of petals in the sun's slow rise.
A flock of starlings glide past the bedroom window,

    then more light, more of what remains,
    sheets spread like wings on the bedroom floor,

the color of our skin once flush, now light as the flesh of pear.
And the arc of stars that flooded the sky last night

    folded into daylight, now clouds, now figuring shapes.
    I turn toward the window and its awakening,

toward feathers shining through the poplar trees,
brightening the strands of your hair, wonder if this is how

    love is released by the body-a brightening stippling the glass,
    a reflection through a window, sheets riddled with our voiceless

struggles by the bedside after they are shaken, opened
by their sudden need, one for the other.

    I lie silent, remembering the vase of wild irises you gave me
    last week, how the buds opened, leaf-split, the willowy violet flags

unfolding, the bent spines darkening. Afterward, the exhaustion
of color and the dark water still greening. When my brother died,

    I watched as the color left him, watched his body arc, then fall silent,
    saw the whitening bruises, wondered, too, if that was love.

I laid orchids on his grave. Lilies. A wreathe of roses spinning silk.
I watched as the color left them, like water drying.

It was the same as when the color left our faces:
Not taken but given. Not stolen but found.

Yesterday, when I saw you at the bathroom sink, a drop of water
streaming toward your elbow, I remembered surrendering

sex, love, beauty, grief, all that is dispersible in the quiet,
remembered leaving the form of what was, astonished and empty,

the vase, the body,
the air before any living thing passed through it.

Coventry

Why has it taken me thirty-two years
to write you this poem?
I had drawer's full of ball point pens I might have used
before they bled themselves dry.

With computers, I'd run out of reasons but not excuses.
I grew up in a household without
having familiar answers to familiar questions,

never learned to question those questioning me.
I kept to myself, my self.
No one knew my poems.

They lived inside my bedroom drawer
alongside my infantry of little green plastic army men.
My grandfather built his house with steel wrists.

My father followed behind him with buckets of nails.
Our construction constituted brimstone
accompanied by exaggerated forms of the masculine—

cul-de-sacs of boats, motor homes, BBQ grills,
roundabouts of the suburban gothic.
There were no thoroughfares.

By the time I'd met you I had clenched teeth and lock jaw.
The last time we saw my grandmother she asked me if I were married.
Her husband had died and left her alone with her thoughts.

I think it's a sin not to be married, not to have children she said.
She had learned to speak without fear, a saving grace of institutionalization.
What more could be done to her I'd reasoned.
We moved her from nursing home to nursing home to nursing home

while she read to us her scripture.
She never spoke of marriage again.

Silence began to frequent our visits more and more.
She grew white.
Who did she think you were all those years?

Rubbing her hands, kissing her cheek, her shadows of carcinoma?
Later, she loved you not knowing why.
We were the boys from the city that no one ever talked about,

who knew all the lyrics to Cole Porter,
you and I, the fun ones, our love born inside ourselves,
our families lost to us years before we arrived.

Timetable

I worry about your penchant for slippers,
your propensity for terry cloth robes
that fall open, the axel of your body.

                    Your hips, your neck that no longer
                    turns independent of your shoulders.
                    Your breath that slips worries me.

A key that turns a lock but won't open.
Last week, there was that surprise bruise
on your arm, the inevitable bloom.

                    Still, you insist on doing everything,
                    lift things you shouldn't—the edge of
                    the sofa a quarter inch, laundry baskets filled

with wet towels. That chair
you moved to the bedroom
shaved a year off your life.

                    I worry about things that haven't happened
                    but are likely to. That I see you often as you were,
                    than are. That I don't see you at all.

You camouflage needle marks with
flesh-colored bandages and don't leave the house,
though I tell you that the world

                    doesn't see anything wrong with you. That
                    solitude is everywhere, that you are not specific
                    enough. None of us are.

Every year, doctors recalculate life expectancy
tables. I shuffle thoughts of when we first met,
chronical summers, shifts of body language.

It's how I learned to love—in fractions,
hundredths, decimals, adding them up.
Calculating subtleties. Multiplying ghosts.

I think if I wait long enough, the past
comes back, reared up on his haunches.
Mouth open, wanting to be fed by hand, by the spoonful.

That it's not in it for the kill.

.Punctuation

a punctuation mark (,) indicating a pause between parts of a sentence. It is also used to separate items in a list and to mark the place of thousands in a large numeral.

1.   *music*
        a minute interval or difference of pitch.

2.   a butterfly that has wings with irregular, ragged edges and typically a white or silver comma-shaped mark on the underside of each hind wing.

I want to be as useful as a comma,
an eyelash
protecting the eye from randomness,

a scythe setting up
my universe for the period,
for the exclamation point,

whichever arrives first batting its wings,
flying through the dark ages.

One eclipse interrupting the next
and the next

onward upward toward
the farthest reaching star
which scientists are still trying to find.

A comma like the Greeks used in history
before they invented history,
carving their destinies

in stone, a drop of rain sliding off the edge
of a leaf deciding whether or not
to plant crops, swallowing the dirt,
turning to roots.

Beethoven's mark in the Ninth Symphony
Adagio, andante, fortissimo
laying his head down, ear to the floor
one sound bending the next.

The dead are always looking up
between rock, up through plants
stopping to remember that they are
the curve of a petal,

a butterfly with useless, ragged edges,
a swath of light wrapped around itself
there before the period, before God
tongue between teeth,

the rim holding onto my last word
marking the place of thousands in a large numeral.
The amount of breath needed
                    before it leaves the body.

My Roots Will Always Be Tangled

I am packed with my suitcases for the long trip and wait in the backseat of my parent's car, quiet as a broken sparrow at night, quiet as the hunted. My head hidden from the eye of the rearview mirror, I prepare for the journey. Now the highway, windows down; wind turns, makes my heartbeat quicken. My body shifts its temperature, my heart, its mooring, birdlike in my cage, wait for an opening, a crack in the window, as a child is set free in a field, or free to pick petals off foxglove, gentian, toss their stems and not be deemed murderous or shameful. As children freed in schoolyards, abandoned barns, amusement parks, but never too free, never far away from the hand that feeds, what covets their movement, as a parent covets with a look or the back of a hand. Shadows covet ground. Trees covet sky.

It is an eighty-six-mile trip, my migration to the mountains that also covet, keep the quiet to themselves, if "themselves" is what you might call them. Once a child names anything, it becomes a person. Capped in snow, with trees that stand as tight as brigades, their tall lean spines not even an arrow can pierce, or a bullet of light, or a child's eyes riding in the backseat of a car, glancing up while coloring. Long silver locks of rivers loosen managed chaos.

We arrive. My parents drive off. I sit on the floor of my grandmother's living room and look up at the grandfather clock whose face is round as a baker. A clock sees everything through a prism. Time is a fragment of spun color, a taste, a rumored smell. Strange furniture broods in corners. The sofa I want to ride. Chairs have arms I long to hold me. The lamp shade-an eyelid that blinks, stutters, that caught my grandmother's own eye when she bought it from the storeowner who didn't know its value, any true value of light, any history of it, this shining through woven thread, like a flashlight shone through a doll house where time is always moving forward through windows, through doors, upstairs, into closets. Nothing changes. In the dark shop, it must have stopped her, changed her- lights little history. As when each morning breaks apart. Suddenly there's a shift in the dark, then all yesterday's pale shadows swept away. Next to this lamp, I sit and ruminate. I know ruminate. I learned it in a spelling bee.

When I am here, I can't remember anything, except that love and stillness can co-exist under the same roof without anyone the lesser for it. I knew even then that sadness ordered a house. Back home, I knew where all the broken dishes were, the chipped glasses. I knew each room marked safe to enter. The thick walls of silence. They, too, raise their armor to fire, cold, to eyes of stars where I see my own reflection and have built my infantry from which I molded my armor. Truth is never apparent. Not what you see, but how you see it, is all. Take fall. For instance, leaves could be dying. It's true. Or they could be awakening to their true color, essences before death when the soul splits, or when a person ages, blisses amplitude, the happiness in a child-head, like rain on skin, the least droplets of rain. And I am scrubbed in wind and brushed dry on grass.

This is my dream. I only want to run. When was the last time you ran, looking at the sky waver like a blue flame? This is my dream. It covets where my toys live and my parents die repeatedly, as parents do when one only remembers the back of a brush. I breathe in this new world- my grandmother's chair, sofa, wall, clock, a ticking that never ceases. Here, love is wired in, stuck like a note to the door of the refrigerator. The made-up mind of a child makes it so. All that glitters is gold when the sealed heart frees, and light enters. I look through my bedroom window at night, the sheets drawn over me, my night wings. I fly in them. Still. And I am always coming home in mind with doors that open wider and wider and wider and wider but open to nothing save darkness of a bedroom floor and a child with a toy truck, yellow as sunlight. A boy turning the sun around him so that he can see through the trees, imitate the hands on the clock and their hours as my mother enters the room, her voice, the sound of strings over the mouth of a red guitar, her lips, that jig-sawed edge.

cubiculum infantium

Dearest, dearest mother,
how does your grey hair grow?

Do your nails chip granite?
Do your hands melt snow?

Have your cheeks bottomed out?
Do your ankles still bloom?

Do they have you shut up
in your hospital room?

What happened to the garden where
the snapdragons pose,

where poison ivy now pickets,
blinding the rose?

Oh mother dear, the dog is dead.
The cat catapulted over the moon.

All the silver's been tarnished
Have you seen that large wooden spoon?

Do you miss your little target?
My arms blown up like balloons?

Do you still smell like powder?
Do you still rub your hands?

How are your legs?
Do they bend like bows?

Dearest, dearest mother,
Do you still fit in your clothes?

There are moments my fingers
trace the shape of your misshapen heart.
It's a start, a start.

Dearest, dearest Mother,
The hands are the hardest to draw.
One made of brick, the other of straw.

Deep love studies to live, to live.
No regrets, my mother's love,
a mourning dove, a mourning dove.

In the Garden Named

She lies on the side of the road. Indifference has left her
unrecognizable in the remnants of her frame.
Her pelt snags the sunlight. Bright, as if her soul hadn't yet
left her, there on the pavement, her body not entirely dissolved
by rain or heat or the steady rhythm of decay. I cannot bring myself
to call the thing "it," so I call it "she" to give her identity,
recognition, a sense of self that once was everywhere
in the Garden named. I imagine she was a mother
at one time who left her brood, kittens perhaps, a nest
of raccoons, eyes opening and closing, tiny yellow windows
waiting for their mother's return, for her mouth of food.
In some species, it is the mother that hunts, the mother
that enters the dark, the mother that does not return.

Last week, I planted bulbs in my garden: forsythia, geraniums,
iris, seeds hard as stones. I soothed them with soil,
the pointed edge of my trowel reverent as a gravedigger,
hollowed space for them to breathe, to open, to bloom,
their roots gathering soil like tiny hands
so when rain falls and summer heat bears down,
they do not dissolve, but come into form, feed on light,
on air before disappearing, leaving their radiance behind.
Nothing disappears, I think. Where something was,
there is something still there. I have not forgotten her,
forgotten where I started and where I was going,
forgotten that blue trick of light I witnessed from her animal body,
her skull on the pavement, the opening seed.

Coming Out to My Mother

I sat at the table
in the full light of the kitchen
while mother stood peeling
apples at the sink.
The oven was on high
and all the windows, wide open.
A fan whirred in the background.
I wanted to turn it off
so I could hear her better,
like when she whispered
"They have a cure for what you have."
I was twelve years old.
She made a sandwich
and set it down in front of me
along with some milk.
Sliding my finger
down the chilled glass,
I drew a circle on the table
and made a little pond.
"May I be excused?" I asked.
It was getting late and
I wanted to be outside
where the birds were,
where they could not be reached.
"May I?"
"Yes," she said.
She untied her apron.
She hung her silence on the door.

Coming Out to My Father

We were sitting on the front porch
and he'd asked me for a smoke.
The air that night was cold.
Our breath hovered between us.
Cigarette ashes drizzled
down the front of his shirt, tapered off.
I told him sometime after mother
had gone upstairs, had gone to bed.
He said, "I love you" and "anyway,"
looked out over the lawn, flicked his
cigarette butt onto the ground
and went inside.
The next day, I studied
how birds built their nests
from broken limbs and lawn scraps,
how they lifted them
into the tree's dark heart
and made them habitable.
I loved my father in his handsome despair,
the loneliness in his eyes,
the chapel I'd entered that night,
and I, wanting only the company of men
When I left for college that summer
we never spoke again.
I was told about his death
two weeks after he died.
By then, my memory
of that night had no shadow.
It had grown that thin.

Remnant Ore

In the town that did not move I grew.
I became the mask landscape wears.
It is here my father grew.
Mornings and evenings I did not see him.

In the town that did not move he grew,
an empty hall. Where love walked I did not
meet him or take his hand. He grew old
and thin in the town where I did not know him.

In the dark weather of my father,
a hollow through a tree.
In the branches of his heart he sang,
in the town that no one knew.

coda iv

It's been suggested that you can live
your life over again if you choose,
or at least parts of it,
in your head,
that you can start anywhere, but where?

A Nightingale's Ode

I am looking out the window and let's say for arguments sake
      that I am the Nightingale Keats sees hopping over blades
           of silk-sullen grass into the morning shade
that has already begun to open like the pages of a book,
and that I am singing to him, forming words in his mouth,
whole passages of night I have saved to ink his red-lined lips,
      which have already begun to shrink, to rot like apples,
         the clouds spreading wings after their restless sleep,
      and the candlelight that shimmers by his bed
a choreography of flight, that the book beside him opened,
dropped off into the day's starlessness, dropped off the feverish flowering
of his body, is now opened again   by the turning sunlight
      dismantling the trees, warming the jasmine curled like fingers
         around the door, returning to the page through the garden,
open-mouthed, bathing his lily-white skin, his body
           unable to hold itself   upright
that it is that wants to make poetry of him
      as he drips in the still white heat of his sheet's mooring, motionless,
as I have sometimes found him, afloat in the center of the room
      like speckled particles of dust giving off ambient light,
         tethering my feathered garment, that it is I that love him,
singing to the soft timpani of his ears each morning joy, joy, joy, joy
as I fly over a pond of glass, the water bristling like the petals of his skin,
      the coppery mosquito, high, high, high up, the brilliant brass plate of the pine,
that it is I now who wait, press my beak against the window,
      peer through the mist of his breath
         to feel the pain of a rose being burned.

Backdraft

I hear
the wind caressing

the backs of flames
as they ride up

the southeasterly
sides of houses,

licking fence posts,
blowing garage doors

open with their blue-white
sacks of tongues,

as if lovers,
bodies ignited,

whisper about
the futility of water.

The new sex talk:
condoms melting on the nightstand,

bottles of lubricant
refueling. The camera

zooms in and everything is quiet,
except the ground,

melting grasshoppers
and wind

tipping up stairs.
The smell of stale cologne

in the air reminds
me of used water.

How like sex, this flash burn.
The day after,

almost beautiful
its cemetery of memory.

Give me another beer
so that I can pretend

it was love,
so that I can pretend

it was passion
that consumed us,

filled us like rain
in desert,

warm wells
in our mouths

to keep us wet,
salt from leaking

from our skin,
our lobes,

at the moment we come
to our senses,

feel the anticipation
of dream-vacation brochures

filled with promising trips
to countries

lit by exotic birds
flying over our bodies,

one-way tickets
with no means

of getting home,
or ever leaving.

Vesper for Integration

When I think about when I last saw you,
I think of the heart that moves

around the house, the senseless heart
and uselessness, Diogenes holding

up a lamp in broad daylight.
The heart that feeds the heart

flown out of itself— a room,
a table, a book opened, pages falling.

I think of the phone that rings,
your voice over the lawn,

carried into the garden's heart,
where I am pounding the soil, sunlight

and senselessness wanting
your hands to pull me

out of my body into yours—
the animal heart

that swallows the heart of its prey,
suddenness torn from the body,

drawing my mouth into your mouth
one breath opening into another,

the iris stalking the heart of the human eye.
I want to wake up flying,

give myself to the heart of wind
the shade of the tree,

an aureole of water
to the lilacs growing in the neighbor's yard.

Take me I want to tell them,
let me open them, swirl inside their mouths

until bees come and carry me away.
Turn me to fall. To spring.

Let me unlatch winter.
Let it fall through my hands.

Blanket me with rain.
Give myself to this heart.

Wrap me in *this* center.
Be the door others walk through.

I want to mark passage,
the heart that never dies.

That First Winter

There are no more remnants of your garden.
Only a few scattered roots lie where the hoe

chipped them, the rake's scratch marks
still faint in the dirt. No more rows

of lettuce leaves quietly curling upward
like saints' hands or beds of tomatoes

ripening in their tight red skins.

The branches of the lemon and the orange tree
are pale, thick and white as bones.

Those hands of yours—
I remember how thick they were,

how the dirt under your fingernails
formed the small arches

our lives would pass through. The house
always smelled of jasmine in the summer.

In the late afternoon, delphiniums
leaned against our bedroom window, made us thirsty.

One day, after an afternoon in the sun,
I watched you as you came inside

to wash your hands and pour yourself
a cold drink of water. You brought

the lip of the glass to your mouth,
sipped like a wild, exotic bird.

I came up from behind,
placed my arm around your shoulder,

kissed your neck,
the tips of your hair.

Sunlight rose through the curtains,
laid down quiet strips on the floor.

Lately, absentmindedly,
I wander from one room to the next

as though looking for something
that I know I will never find.

I open a drawer. Straighten your mother's
wingback chairs. I would have thought myself

alone, except that every few moments
I think I hear a cough, and the cat

go gunshot through the hallway.

Nothing but the cold makes sense.
I let it in through a crack in the backdoor.

I like the way it moves around the house,
climbs the walls where my favorite picture

of you hangs. Remember?
You were twenty-five, and light

from the sun fell over your face

startling everything.

Ceremony

I see the old every day

       sitting behind their picture windows

looking out at what they left behind—

                     summer clothes, summer skin,

shoes in one hand,   and running,

       now bare-boned, hands folded,

        now leaving.

We're all where we used to be, once flown, surrendered.

                We remember her. She was always smiling,

      the nurses said about my grandmother

as she sat in the dining room

      listening to them running,

balancing pills, holding paper cups of water.

They told me to keep talking to her,

      that in a body dying hearing fades the slowest.

And when I told my grandmother

      I was here, she squeezed my hand.

What I want to believe:

      She was holding on

to the house in which she grew,   to the window, to the moon that held her awake,

      to the tree she climbed

      hidden in the branches, to her body flying.

It wasn't the dying her hands told me.

      It was the holding on to, looking back

over the room, the bed, the sheets, the open door,

her body white,   light piercing skin on her hands.

II.

My mother and father were the cathedrals I prayed in.

I took to myself,

     held words,
          rolled them over and over
  slap   *kick*   *scream*   *cry*

dropped through my fingers,   became my bruised consensus.

I paraded around the house in my sister's clothes,

      exhausted words like should and sorry,
        played with dolls.

Unusual sweetness developed early, made me lonely
              until shirts, ties and polished shoes
fed my father's ambition.

    There was flying in the yard once   *fence*   *wall*
      when my arms knew possibility,
          flapping around the front yard,

when I understood the word *dream*—

                              past desire and other reasons.

Now my mouth gated shut, latched.

          Whoever turned the clock forward,

                         the second hand is off.

When you're buried they dress you up in a suit and a respectable tie,

interlock your fingers,

              splay your hands over your chest

                              like unanswered prayers.

I don't know what happened in my late stages,

              why I dressed myself for a life I had no interest in.

You need thrown at me from all directions.

              Clouds outside. The sky's chapel.

I go to the graveyard   listen to my father twist the words in my head.

                                    to light from hallway swept

               under   door jamb

to closet   of perfect quiet

        where I wait with eyes closed,

              listen to waves turn, gulls cry,

                  where a back-hand lands

above the upper struts of a jaw   and a wild blue nerve

                                  opens to an ocean.

coda v

Animals make themselves heard.
They give noise away.
This is how they survive,
this, the singing among them,
a hunger for a kind of love that is ecstatic,
a territory unguarded.

But for the Way They Breathe

In the churchyard I lay down a map of myself,
spread beneath the tree—
corners taut, held down by stones,
a shadow taunting light, burying leaves.

You cannot live with grief too long, a poet said.
So I am here that I might carry sorrow better,
hum, think, my shoes fingerprint grass,
my hands stuff coat pockets to keep warm.

Past headstones I walk, pay homage, kneel,
my one brother's absence nearly twenty years,
another brother's nearly as much, he the same age as me.
Drafts of sparrows swarm porticos of light,

flood the narrowing hallways of trees,
break the silence with their winter psalms.
A burst of cold air shuffles through me, rises upward.
I don't know where it comes from or from whom.

My parents always had something to say,
now breaths I brush against that I might hear
what I did not know and know what I did not hear,
to touch what touches me, to listen a thousand times.

Hands clasped behind my back, I recite the prayer
I studied in Sunday school, as if I were saying it
for the first time—my ears, an audience to vowels
rounded by nerves, missed words, adolescence.

It is the best of who I was then, unstudied, open as a book.
Each year I return, human to human, to mark ones I love,
an envoy of stories, I tell my family what I've been up to,
ask them how they are feeling, talk about all the things

we talked about when they were alive—the office, weather,
politics, how short life is, how all of us wished we'd had more time.
I have found the dead never tire of the ordinary.
And the more stories I tell them, the more alive

they become, ascending into cold morning air
like smoke from a wood-burning stove.
Sunlight climbs the foot of a nearby tree, a bow over leaves,
which remind me of a kind of instrument, a kind of heaven.

An emerald coat pulls up its mottled sleeves.
I shift the ground beneath my feet, seasonal changes
I no longer wish to brush away—browned reds,
curled nests of hybrid yellows, my hands ferried

across names washed away by rain, as smooth
as the features of a monument.
I would wipe away the cobwebs
but for the light they carry,

the way they breathe.

Burning the Field

It's 1985. I am angry with God.
Nancy changes hairdressers.
No one knows where Ronnie is.
Rock Hudson and Doris Day make a public appearance.
Rock does not know how ill he looks.
Tall, thin, elegant, he smiles
for cameras as he was trained to do.
He dies with fanfare, a translucent Doris beside him.
In the end, even France cannot save him.
Doris continues to groom her dogs,
smooth her skin with Vaseline.
At ninety, she is as beautiful as the French Riviera.

***

How do I make *this* beautiful?
The dying don't want to let go of anyone's hands.
Bodies are carried out of hospitals with unpatrolled frequency.
My brother and I die together,
though I watch him die first.
Death is an arrival, a departure.
But a departure from whom, an arrival from what?
Present, perfect, past, pluperfect; all love's indicatives rally.
Address books become memorabilia of the dead.

***

My mother tells me as she irons
that AIDS is God's will,
her truth, simple, her conscience, immaculate.
If it is God's will, I say, why does he kill children?
She keeps ironing as if she were trying to make
the crease in her jeans permanent.
For years we do not know how to speak to one another.

***

The government states
that there are geographical limits to grief.
Volunteers construct a quilt to administer loss.
Breezes pull threads, pick glitter.
Potted chrysanthemums circle a patchwork
of names, fragments of sun-stained faces.
Top layers appear in shades of lipstick
mothers and sisters wore.
Like the walls of old frescoes
they fade more and more each year.

***

Studious in its grief, the world, on bright sunny yellow days,
lays my brother out as a sort of commemorative
alongside the thousands that came before
him and that are still arriving,
washed ashore like the war dead.
A field that flourishes every year,
a garden the public never grows tired of:
death, colors, numbers, their ability to astonish.
There have always been enthusiasms for the intangible.
In the end, my brother stretches fifty miles.

***

When birds quiet,
and the hallowed yellow weather wanes,
panels are folded one atop the other,
plump as rain-soaked telephone directories,
stored in water-tight bins
the size of small animals.
Lights along the National Mall, dim.
Who is remembered is forgotten,
who was forgotten, remembered.
Stars scatter across the surface of the water.
The reflecting pool calms by degrees.

***

Today, survivors hold out
in overpriced condominiums,
misshapen by cures,
cocktails the color of persimmon.
No pictures dwell on side tables,
populate cream-colored walls.
No one wants to know how they got here.
There is so much more silence between words.
There is so much more drinking.
 Activists fled to retirement communities
years ago, shuttered in like silent film stars.
You can see their fingertips parting the blinds.

***

In 2018, a man in Georgia said get out of my
house with all that gay and poured boiling
water over two boys caught sleeping
together in the same bed.
I'd like to say that neither of them
were hurt severely, that they ended up
being released from the hospital,
that they are home, fine, loved.
He burned their lips off.

Unmooring

Unmoor me from this dream, the sheet's mooring;
My head from this pillow, unmoor its sinking,
my hair from its tethered scrawl.

Unmoor my body from the mattress,
my fingers from the sunlight's glove.
From this shower, the water's beaded mooring of my hair.

Screw the cap off this bottle,
the lid off this tube, uncover the cover from this jar.
Unmoor the light from this window.

Like a boat, the white, white sail,
unmoor my destination, let me arrive in an onslaught
of unchartered air. The car from the garage, its dark moor,

the darkest part, pull it from its slumber,
the key, the handle, the lock, the door.
Unmoor me from the driveway, the flow of traffic,

the river of faces moored to the windshield, to taillights
flickering on the asphalt, to the red, red glaze.
The pavement, unmoor it too.

Peel it like the skin of an apple,
then unmoor its core. Unmoor my eyes
from the road, the stoplights. The Stop Sign,

unmoor it from the corner, fences from fence posts, gates.
Here let go the housekeeping bee, here, the laddering vine.
Unmoor the children in the crosswalk.

Let them walk in the trees, then unmoor the trees.
Let them walk in the clouds, then unmoor the clouds.
Let rivers rise up and over the ground

Let the sound of the waterfall
Let go of the stars
You never owned them to begin with

They were never yours
Let go of the wind through your fingers
What held you to it and it to you like water like rain.

You're falling still.
Hold all the petals to your face
Hold the dying.

Look at them through the iris of your eye
It's here they burn inside you
It's here you never leave.

Essential

I am a grocery clerk,
an essential worker inside a pandemic
that will kill me if I return to back
to the person
I was two months ago.
I circumvent crowded aisles,
estimate distances.
There are fewer and fewer spaces
for me to move into.
I wear masks and gloves that will keep me alive,
no longer recognize myself in the mirror.
No one knows who I am.

My co-workers and I huddle around the timeclock.
A fingerprint announces our arrival.
There are rules about tardiness.
Our shifts are long.
We are poured through an hourglass.
Hola chula. Hola guapo. Hola huero.
I learn that *huero* means white boy in Spanish.
Customers assume I am the store manager
though all of us wear masks.
You look like a store manager they say.
I don't understand why they assume this
and I do understand why they assume this.
I am *huero*, the language they want to hear.

Mateo is sixty-five, cleans toilets in our public restroom.
He picks up used syringes and needles
left by customers who park their mobile homes
and minivans in our parking lot.
He has worked for the grocery store for thirty years
and makes twelve dollars and seventy-five cents an hour.
During breaks, he takes his shoes off, rubs
the bottoms of his feet,
shows me his callouses.
The other day I heard him crying.

I think about my mother.
She taught me that Hispanics were dirty and stupid,
that they were lazy.
My mother never worked a job in her life,
died in a trailer park with no money.
Her attributes were earned poverty
living the good life at no fault of her own.
Before she died, she mailed her crucifix to me.

I bring my own lunch, sit by myself.
The break room is filled with my silence.
I listen to the others,
pick up on words I learned in high school:
necessito, trabajando, malo.
I learn how to piece lives together.
They will never know mine.
My church taught me to hate myself early on.
I am a homosexual,
a world buried inside another inside another
for as long as I can remember,
good at what I do.
I keep myself to myself.
I can't unlearn the language I was born into.
Language that no one spoke aloud.
In Muslim countries,
we are still tossed from the tops of buildings.

 Constance works for sixteen-fifty an hour.
She is a manager and has twenty years with the company.
I just started, make seventeen dollars an hour,
one of three *hueros*
out of one hundred and thirty Hispanics.
Everyday, she asks me how I am.
Everyday, I say *fine, okay.*
In English, these words are effortless.
They have no meaning.

Angela in the Deli Department died two months ago.
She wasn't feeling well one day and never came back to work.
Her picture is taped to the bulletin board by the timeclock
with the caption "sunrise and sunset."
She smiles beatifically at the camera.
She is young, beautiful.
Six months have passed.
No one will take her picture down.
Richard, who worked with her for years,
tells me the doctors found a lump on his neck,
that he needs to see a doctor,
but keeps pushing back his appointment.
I can't afford it, he says.
I have a wife and two kids.

Marta is sixty-five years old, bags groceries,
collects shopping carts in the parking lot
in one-hundred-degree weather.
She is invisible to the public.
Since the virus, I have not seen her.
Goodbyes seldom accompany disappearances.
Last year she took all the money she had and flew to
Paris with her family.
She brought me back a key chain.
It holds the keys that opens every door I enter
and re-enter thousand-fold.
Her absence is everywhere.

Ana works in the floral department—
tulips, orchids, roses—
arranges and rearranges color,
measures the length of stems—
Get well. Sorry for your loss.
Bows becomes signatures to the dead.
Orchids gather at the front entrance,
float in sunlight like swans on a lake.

When do you need them by Ana asks.
I'm sorry to hear that.
For her there are no hours.

Alejandro stocks the water aisle. He is fifty-five
and has massive arms and shoulders.
How are you honey, he says to me.
He is part Puerto Rican, part French.
He always smiles when I talk to him.
I know, I know, I know.
I can't tell if he understands me
or if I understand him.
He works in the aisles,
keeps to himself, barely speaks,
his back, torn by long hours
and past surgeries.
Everywhere he goes a part
of his language goes missing.

Early morning, customers arrive
in Range Rovers and old Meredes,
compete for limited parking.
Their hair is perfect.
They balance their steps.
I used to kiss the old women on the cheek.
I now nod my head,
stand as far away from them as possible.
They have less then than know,
that they can dream of.
There hours are short.
Their language, dying.

Week after week we wait—
Mi familia, abuela, hermano, hermana
for accounting to complete payroll
so that we know what we

will have left of ourselves,
scheduled into the future,
days and weeks that take our selves
out of ourselves.

We walk out to the parking lot,
take off mask so that we can breathe.
Every day they leave scars on our face,
cover our fear. Everyday,
we touch something that will kill us.
Our language turns to silence.
Our conversations disappear.

Self-Quarantine

A match, a tank of kerosene,
    I sit around gaslighting past lives in my head
like when I was eleven,
    rode my bicycle to the store,
stole a pack of cigarettes,
    burned holes in the air.
And there's my father,
    the Vietnam War,
TV coughing up blood
    my mother burning holes in her throat
while I set fire to old family photographs
    tilt them downward
so that they burn faster.
    By noon, high school is up in flames —
potential wind gusts
    of up to 80 miles per hour
expected to last for years.
    Then a photo. Then scorched earth. Then nothing.
Flame throwers clear
    my first time in bed with a man
when I thought sex and love
    were the same thing,
that it would take a lifetime before
    I would know the difference.
Bombs fall where my twin brother died,
    turn everything I know about love
into ash that reignites itself
    before I go to bed each night –
fuses in my arm, nurses, doctors,
    my body burning from the inside out.
Tomorrow's shave at the bathroom sink
    another war staring back
at me with a mouthful of grenades,
    ready to pull the pin,
        breathing fire,
            hauled up out of nowhere,
                hauled up from a well.

Fresh Kill

I wish I'd known something
of beauty
before the world wrote prescriptions for it—
better skin, hair,
and too bad you're not taller.

When I was little, I stood
in front of my bathroom mirror
already searching for someone I wasn't,
with a hairbrush in my hand,
my microphone into my future,

wanting to become myself
before the world stepped in,
yanked me aside
to take a better look.
When did I stop screaming for something I wanted?

Rachmaninoff rushing the shore with his baton,
That. That. Nooo. Thaaaaaaaaaat.
I don't run around in public anymore,
arms flailing, failing, finger paint houses, chimney smoke,
swing from illuminated trees.

I don't blow out dandelions.
There are no longer balloons tied to my wrist
or grown-ups bending down
to tell me how beautiful I am.
A lion drinks from the muddy bank of a river,

a cub follows and so it goes for generations
roaming the Sahara looking for water,
a safe place to sleep and fresh kill.
Now me with my oeuvre of haircuts; trafficking in ties,

exfoliating my youth with a razor,
too quiet, envying stars,
mirrors like funhouses throwing back at me
that little boy who became my father
who once cried in public,

raised his hand in front
of the bathroom mirror and sang.
I wish I could wrap my mirror around
me, find myself with a tail,
wings sprouting from my shoulder,
breathing fire,

loving myself, loving him.

Dear Bettye Blythe Francis

I'm guessing that you are the same Bettye Blythe Francis I knew in college at Indiana University in Bloomington in the late '70's and early 80's. I'm guessing that you are the

same Bettye Blythe Francis I drove home to Wabash occasionally to spend a weekend with your parents on my way home to Fort Wayne to visit mine. I'm guessing that you are the

same Bettye Blythe Francis I first met on a weekend in August of 1975 forty-seven years ago driving to Bloomington to see the opera "Carmen" with Hal Brown whom I worked with at

Camp Big Island where our Boy Scout troop stayed that year and almost baked for the heat. I'm guessing that there are not that many Bettye Blythe Francises around still living, and so

I'm taking a chance that you are that same person. I'm guessing you're the Bettye Blythe Francis who befriended me and I'm writing this now because we're both getting older and

I've been thinking about you for about forty-seven years and wondering how it happened that we lost contact with one another and how the years flew by and how I never said to you

the things I'm saying to you now, what you meant to me, how much I loved you—as I sit at my kitchen table and look out over the street and listen to birds think. I see you standing

near the campus library as I last remember you, holding your books, one hand blocking the sun from your eyes, your long shadow on the lawn spinning and turning color, the leaves

falling as they did every year, as they're doing now, effortlessly, and the sudden wind with all its memories curling the lip of your dress, tousling the tips of your hair, remembering

how when I left Bloomington in August of 1985 to move to California, it was sudden—not planned—the alertness of it, and how I had temporarily lost my mind over another boy,

ignored my friends and not remembering if I said goodbye or if we were on good terms or bad at that point or if we had just drifted apart as is so often the case with friendships with love, running aground as I was, so much trying to catch up on things, things I thought significant—furniture, a new coffee maker, what to keep, what to throw away—not

understanding that everything I was leaving behind was what I needed to take with me, the nights we spent on the steps of the dorm, gossip from our mouths rising like smoke, each

looking up at the brightness of the moon as only someone our age could see it, the white flame of it in the darkness, in the winter, the morning, when the sun rose, and we both

stood beautiful in the earth's ease, in her bright blaze of color, our shadows disappearing in the simple way that two people disappear into life. Remember the Great Lakes? We

thought they were oceans. I'm guessing you're still there, because I need to remember you as I knew you then, feeling the wind. I'd like to think that our time here on this earth is

ultimately undisturbed, that when we enter it, it closes behind us, a place without despair, a beginning, an endlessness played: October, the maple's red hands, spring rain signing the

grass, and the two of us still alive in this world, tucking in bed sheets, somewhere laughing, laughing like waves.

Thesaurus

when evenings come and go   when flowers fold and dark waits   for something to happen
on water   when mornings come and go   windowless mornings
without sky   sunlight emptied   all over the lawn
when words   don't come anymore   easy words   that came from somewhere once
listing themselves onto the blank pages   of your bodies   like riding a bus
with all its bright intimacy   mouths, eyes closed, vowels sliding down
the back of your throat   what do you do with silence   glance out a window
walk around neighborhoods   watch leaves oscillate and white roses
bloom preternaturally in dark   while you wait for someone who isn't there
to fill a living room   once known   a lover at the kitchen table
someone you knew once   loved once   still known
an empty chair beside the fireplace   that picture in the hallway you drift by
year after year   the one that's too close   for your eyes to
examine   when everything flowed at once   when you were young
and everything fell easy

like rain, like petals

Oranges & Sardines

Last night we stayed home.
Last night we stayed home again.
Last night you drank scotch, watched TV.
And we stayed home again.

Last night I looked at you in the half light.
Your head up, you held your scotch.
We stayed home again, watched TV
I watched you lift your glass.

I saw your mother in your eyes.
We talked when the movie stopped.
We stayed home again last night.
I was looking for something.

I was looking for something to say.
About the woman in the movie we were watching.
And the man she looked at without words.
Sometimes, I look at you without looking for something.

They were watching TV, this man, this woman.
They held hands, I held yours.
It was your mother's hand so it was mine.
It was your father's hand so it was mine.

Last night we stayed home.
Last night we stayed home again.
Last night you drank scotch, we watched TV.
I sipped from a glass of red wine.

The scotch was brilliant,
the color of oranges & sardines,
flickering in the flickering light.
We stayed home again, last night, last night, last night.

Tomorrow again, the grey, grey light,
will hang like a bracelet, a loom, a loom.
That grey light I sometimes see you in.
But it doesn't matter now in our bed, in this room, this room.

Last night we stayed home, again.
Last night you drank scotch, we watched TV.
I drank from your glass, orange & sardines.
The scotch spun, I held your hand.

I am looking for something to say,
About the woman in the movie we were watching.
And the man she looked at without words.
I remember what that couple remembered about themselves.

The scotch spun oranges, the TV sardines.
Lights off, socks on, I kissed you,
our bodies, shape shifting pails of sand,
silence rubbing away our names and our voices,

We stayed at home again, last night, two owls.
Your hair is the color of fine scotch, mine, sardines.
How wise we've become perched aloft in our feathered bed.
Last night we remember, everything about ourselves, said.

Millennium

We stood on the shore
wind blowing
a flock of gulls
fastened above our heads
and flapped our arms
along the water's edge
a pair of pterodactyls
circling
our skin
white where we grabbed
each other's arm
laughed
our swimsuits
sliding down our hips
backs to the sun
pyramids
huge on the water
and centuries passed
and the water
over our feet
bubbled
broke apart
and the sun lifted
our shadows
over the ocean
let us go

A FLOODING OF THOUGHT
A Conversation between Mitchell Untch and Jerrod Schwarz

Mitchell, let me start off by saying what a joy it has been to work on this collection with you, and we feel so honored to publish it. I want to start our discussion off by diving headfirst into one of the major concerns of the book: family. Specifically, Memorial with Liminal Space investigates how our families exist far outside of their physical selves, and our memories of them are often just as concrete as their bodies. What were the challenges and joys of writing so intimately about family? Over these hundred poems, what surprised you?

I think you travel with family your entire life. As you get older perspectives may change but the core imprint remains with you., i.e., were you loved, or not, were you held by your parents, and conversely, did you love them, did you hold them close? Exploring these ideas through poetry can help you gain perspective as to why you behave the way you do and what motivates you as a human being.

Following that line of thinking, how has your perspective about family changed? What stands out as the biggest evolution from your first poems about family to now?

The psychological imprints that your childhood brings stays with you your entire life. As I get older I grow more into myself. The trick is, no matter how you are raised, that you learn to grow from your experiences and create something beautiful from them. I don't want to live a tragedy; I want to live a life of hope and encouragement. Shakespeare's tragedies are sublimely beautiful. There's no hatred there. There's no animosity. It's all exploration. It's all a diving into the human soul.

These poems are dense and lyrical, often going multiple pages and covering a lot of ground. I've been an editor for nearly 10 years, and I have seen the undulating trends around long poems and the push for shorter works that can be more accessible for social media. What draws you to write longer poems? What do your first drafts look like in comparison?

I believe that poems ultimately write themselves. I never sit down with the idea of writing a long or short poem. I simply allow my imagination to take hold and take me as far as it wants to take me.

In several of my rural poems, I write about what I observe. Nature is filled with extraordinary diversity, intimacy, and discovery, which is another way to say that there is great poetry inherent in the observation of it. Everything I observe draws out of me an emotional response. During the editing process I try to bring as much specificity to my work as possible. Intimacy is captured through specificity. I must be inside the poem in order to write about it in any meaningful way.

I really like that connection between intimacy and specificity, especially the admission that it comes about in editing. What does your editing process look like? How different are your first and final drafts?

Sometimes a poem can go through several drafts. Sometimes they arrive after only a couple of drafts. You can always improve upon a work of yours, because as writers were always learning, were always growing. There's probably not a writer alive that hasn't looked back at a work of there's only to find areas that can be improved on. It's part of growth. I've learned to write with humility.

Many of these poems exist at the intersection of faith and mortality. I love the moments in this collection where the speaker splays open spirituality as both a flawed, painful ruleset and as a necessary, metaphysical comfort. I'm curious to know if this subject matter is in all of your writing, or just this collection? As a writer, what about faith most interests you?

I believe that spirit inhabits the physical. If we are at our core spiritual, we cannot be flawed. I am not a religious person, nor do I follow any religious indoctrination. For me, a thought gets its root from a culmination of our personal knowledge, experience and understanding of life, a fluid process to say the least. From this culmination, I explore my faith and understanding of life through poetry. For me, Rilke's writings seek this essential struggle for understanding the why, who and what we are.

Rilke is surely one of the rare poets who has had nearly constant staying power in the minds of every new generation of writers. What draws you to Rilke? Additionally, who are some other poets that have had a big impact on your writing?

When I read Rilke, I feel a kind of ecstatic beauty. To me, it's as if he's allowing his stream of consciousness to take precedent. A flooding of thought, if you will. And isn't that the trick? To make poetry seem effortless? The irony of course is that we know that it does take effort! I've read a lot of poets over the years. My bookshelves at home are crammed with other poets works. I think it's healthy to read a wide variety of poets, as well as other great writers. If you study painting, where do you go? Museums. I started reading Shakespeare when I was seventeen. From there, I read Balzac, Zola, Solzhenitsyn, Chekov, etc. I made flash cards for all the words I didn't know or understand at the time I was reading them. Great fiction can seem like great poetry. All great writing informs the writer, no matter what they choose to write. I became a poet later in life. Of course, Whitman had a great impact. Other more contemporary poets like Sharon Olds, Adrienne Rich. Ann Carson, Yusef Komunyakaa, Gerald Stern, etc., proved to be invaluable.

ACKNOWLEDGEMENTS

Thank you to the following presses for first publishing these poems:

"The Unmooring," *The Aurorean*, 2011

"Elegy," "Psalm," *Badlands*, 2019

"But for the Way They Breathe," *Chattahoochee Review*, 2016

"Leviticus," *Chicago Quarterly*, 2018

"Vesper for Integration," *Chiron Review*, 2019

"Twin III," *Cimmaron Review*, 2022

"Twin I & 2," *The Cleaver*, 2022

"Anatomy," "Gertrude," "Nightingale's Ode," *Confrontation*

"Eden," *Quiddity*

"Essential," *Evening Street Review*, 2020

"Evolution 1," *The Wax Paper*, 2022

"Grey Sparrow," *Family Hymn (Hymn)*, 2014

"Social Distancing," *Fjords*, 2021

"Punctuation," "Self-Quarantine," *I-70*, 2020

"Coventry," "Walking Backwards," *Illuminations*, 2019, 2020

"Better Angels," "Better Angels II," *Massachusetts Review*, 2019

"Dear Bettye Blythe Francis," *Poet Lore*, 2016

"But For The Way They Breathe, *Chattahoochee Review*, 2016

"Before the Wedding," *Saranac Review* 2015

"Ceremony," *Silk Road*, 2022

"West Trade Review," *Anniversary*, 2021

"How Did I Come Here?" *South Dakota Review*, 2012

"Burning the Field," *srpr*, 2020

"Fresh Kill," *The American Journal of Poetry*, 2020

"Beautiful," *The Big Windows Review*, 2021

"Backdraft," *Tar River Poetry*, 2018

"That First Winter," The Tishman Review, 2017

"Remnants of a Solitary Walker," *The Tule Review*, 2017

"Coming Out-Mother, Coming Out-Father," "Solitary Confinement,"
        West Trade Review, 2019

THANKS

I would like to thank my very first poetry instructor Laurel Ann Bogen for my early years of instruction and for allowing me the freedom to explore my writing skills without judgement and always with a great amount of encouragement. I'd also like to thank Molly Bendall for her contribution to my work as both a friend and as an invaluable editor. Many thanks to Spencer Reece, Richard Blanco, Suzanne Lummis, Maril Crabtree, Jami McCarty, the staff at Driftwood Press, Justin Hargett, Maria Pavone, Carol Frost, my partner, Richard Lancaster, who endures all of my idiosyncrasies and insecurities as a poet and as a person, Gloria Lane who taught me how to sing, my deceased twin brother Dana, who lives with me every time I look in a mirror, take a breath, Myra Humphrey, Jami McCarty, Lise Goett, Christine Jonas, June Harris, my brother Martin Scott, Dan Verette, and everyone who, while writing this, I forgot to mention, but who lives inside me and encourages me with their love and wisdom.

Mitchell Untch is an emerging writer. Partial publications include *Beloit Poetry Journal, Poet Lore, North American Review, Confrontation, Nimrod Intl, Natural Bridge, Owen Wister, Solo Novo, Knockout, Baltimore Review, Lake Effect, The Catamaran Reader; Grey Sparrow, Illuminations, Tusculum Review, Telluride Institute, West Trade Review, Wax Paper, Crab Orchard Review* Book Contest Semi-finalist 2017, *Orison* First Book Contest 2017 Finalist, and a two-time Pushcart Nominee.

CPSIA information can be obtained
at www.ICGtesting.com
Printed in the USA
JSHW051909090423
39986JS00002B/12